THE CITY OF MAN

A Declaration on World Democracy

THE CITY OF MAN

A Declaration on World Democracy

Issued by

Herbert Agar

Frank Aydelotte

G. A. Borgese

Hermann Broch

Van Wyck Brooks

Ada L. Comstock

William Yandell Elliott

Dorothy Canfield Fisher

Christian Gauss

Oscar Jászi

Alvin Johnson

Hans Kohn

Thomas Mann

Lewis Mumford

William Allan Neilson

Reinhold Niebuhr

Gaetano Salvemini

THE VIKING PRESS · NEW YORK

1941

2824

CONTENTS

THE CITY OF MAN

PUBLISHERS' NOTE

The origin of the following documents is fully explained in the Note at the end of the volume. Here it need only be said that they are the outcome of the collective thinking of a group of persons profoundly concerned about the future of our civilization in the face of the immeasurable dangers threatening it today. It is a statement of their faith and hope.

Declaration

"A PROCESS OF CHANGE THAT
has lasted for thousands of years is approaching its
completion. Man's solar period is coming to its
end." This is the prophecy ascribed to Hitler. This
has been his deed.

The summer solstice of 1940 saw Europe's solar
period come to its end, the Continent overrun by the
Nazi armies, France smitten and dismembered, and
the Mediterranean drawn into the whirlpool by the
Fascist pirate. Nor was there anything to comfort
our sight farther east, from the obscurity of Russia
to the agony of China.

The entire Old World, where our forefathers lie
and whence all life and light came to us, sinks in a

[11]

catastrophe unequaled in the record of man. For the Huns were but a brief hurricane and their chieftain Attila could even listen to the entreaties of a holy man. The barbarians of the early Middle Ages were eager to learn in the school of Christ and Rome. But nothing is holy to their successors of our day, and the lawlessness of power is their only law.

The peace they promise would be more terrifying than the war they wage. No refuge would be spared. The arm of totalitarianism is long enough to reach into the anchorite's desert.

On the eve of America's declaration of war in 1917, Wilson said: "The wrongs against which we now array ourselves are no common wrongs; they cut to the very roots of human life." These words sound even more compelling to us now. For the conquerors of today have openly set before man the goal of nihilism. "I shall eradicate the thousands of years of human domestication," said Hitler. "I want to see again in the eyes of youth the gleam of the beast of prey. A youth will grow up before which the world will shrink."

[12]

England, where modern man first rose to his dignity, still holds out in tragic valor—a bastion in flames. But not even her survival in heroic self-defense would be adequate, without outside help, to the task of reshaping a world; and the alternative of defeat has been ominously intimated by her Premier himself—"until," he said, "in God's good time, the New World, with all its power and might, sets forth to the liberation and rescue of the Old."

This New World cannot be identified with the Western Hemisphere, a geographical concept not yet matured as a symbol of steadfast unity, a house still divided and exposed both to attack from without and to erosion within.

The New World, if any, is the United States—now faced with an isolation of which no isolationist ever dreamed. With its natural allies in the Old World stricken or dead, with scattered elements of the European empires gravitating around it for protection, and with the Latin-American republics more in need of succor than likely to provide any as

[13]

long as progressive leadership among them is threatened by totalitarian conspiracy, it is this country virtually alone that carries man's burden—the heir to all civilization if England falls, the leader and healer if England endures and bleeds.

An immediate war of "liberation and rescue" seems an absurd assignment. But more absurd is the design for America to crawl behind her ditches in a pretended self-sufficiency like Byzantium in the Dark Ages, in the delusion of a permanent separation, which would be slow death, or in the hope that the European victors might wait for "God's good time" to come, leaving to America the choice of the moment for her war of rescue.

There is no compromise or truce in the totalitarian mind, and as it takes two to be at war it takes two to be at peace. Whether and when we may be called to actual battle may still lie hidden in the alternatives of the impending future. But the major choice is no longer ours. War, declared or undeclared, actual or virtual, has chosen us.

Forerunners of Nazi Germany, as early as forty-odd years ago, anticipating the great wars, had said already: "Some months after we finish our work in Europe we will take New York." The Nazi conquerors today manifestly envision the time, not God's good time, when they will be "ready to take the stride into overseas space."

The awakening of America in 1940 was as tumultuous as the dream of gratuitous peace had been deep. Aid to France and England, short of war, became a password—too late for France, at least—and unprecedented plans of armaments were rushed before the nation—late although not too late if hearts are behind the arms. No error is deadlier than to ascribe the conquerors' victories to their superiority in technology alone, with the inference that a mightier mechanical equipment could redress by itself the wrongs of a mechanical destiny. They were stronger in arms because they were stronger in heart. It was their fanatical faith that gave them wings and fire; it was the singleness of their purpose that sharpened the spearheads of their march.

To the compactness of their religion of darkness the rulers of France and England had nothing to oppose but a dim, Hamlet-like glow. The blindness of their diplomacy and the helplessness of their strategy were the external symptoms of a decay of the soul. Lip-service to conventional ideals went together with delay and evasion; nay, with surrender and treason. This they called appeasement. It implied the conviction that no conviction is worth fighting for and that the boundaries between good and evil had fallen. Military defeat was the outcome of moral abdication.

This country too had gone a long way toward appeasement and confusion. It had discriminated between Fascism and Nazism, thus encouraging the Fascist vulture to make ready for its swoop on the Nazi battlefield. It had supplied Japan with arms and ammunition while lamenting the fate of China. It had deserted republican Spain and perverted neutrality into connivance with the aggressor, thus

[16]

lending a hand to the encirclement of France and to the rise, on Europe's shores and isles, of military threats against ourselves.

These were tragic errors. More tragic, and the cause of them all, was the plight of democracy among ourselves. Democracy had been a strenuous unity of thought and action, a rule for life and death. We were now making of it a "way of life," smooth to the heart's content. It had been a faith militant and triumphant. It was now disintegrating into a routine of "liberties and comforts." To the frustrated masses who felt the meaning draining out of life, the ruling classes promised a coming age of plenty, with rising standards of living. Poverty and insecurity remained, but our mechanical prowess, with its millions of gadgets, was the answer to the ancient needs of man.

An education adrift in a relativity that doubted all values, and a degraded science that shirked the spiritual issues and promised all material delights while withholding the fulfillment of the promise in the mirage of an ever-imminent future, did not lull the masses into tranquillity. They were goaded to despair.

The despair of the masses needs only ruthless leadership to become the revolt of the masses. The leadership was provided in the Old World. The emptiness of man's heart was filled with the pride of the conquering horde or with the slumber of the enslaved herd, and today mass-man, rootless man, has been summoned to the destruction of the civilization by which he had been betrayed. There are no rules in this battle, and there is no pity. A stricken world is seeking to obliterate itself.

The doom of the Old World will be our doom unless we make a last stand. There is only one defense. Unless our world is to die, "self-slain on its own strange altar," we must renew the faith and the hope that once made us strong.

The signers of this manifesto neither bid for power nor shrink from responsibility. They are a group who have wished to devote their lives to the work of the mind. They believe that the time has

[18]

come when the isolation of the intellectual from the body politic, which has cursed both thought and action during the last generations, must be deliberately broken down.

Whether heralds of the Antichrist, from Machiavelli to Nietzsche, or irresponsible artists and scientists masking their egoism as inviolate beauty and esoteric truth, thousands of intellectual leaders or misleaders have been guilty of bringing on the present catastrophe no less than the ruling classes and statesmen, who were their pupils.

None of us or of our contemporaries can escape some share of this blame, for we have all to some degree accepted this culture and immersed ourselves in it. This recognition of guilt must pave the way, not to maudlin regrets, but to immediate atonement.

The present peril and challenge we must accept, in the spirit of Milton, as an ordeal by tyranny.

> Tyranny must be,
> Though to the tyrant thereby no excuse.
> Yet sometimes nations will decline so low

[19]

From virtue, which is reason, that no wrong,
But justice, and some fatal curse annex'd,
Deprives them of their outward liberty,
Their inward lost.

To this expiation by tyranny, now already an accomplished fact over a large expanse of the world, we oppose the ancient dream of man, which we deem imperishable. In an era of Apocalypse we call for a Millennium.

And, first of all, we reaffirm that the meaning and goal of human life, individual and collective, are progress and growth in intellect and action, and that peace, universal peace, is the prerequisite of progress and growth. We realize that man's effort is endless and that no perfectibility leads to an ultimate and unchangeable perfection for mankind to live in happily ever after. Millenniums, to be sure, are the infinity of man's dream enclosed in brief myths, and each horizon opens into another. For "it is provided in the very essence of things," as Walt Whitman has said, "that from any fruition of success, no matter what, shall come forth something to make a greater struggle necessary."

> All experience is an arch wherethro'
> Gleams that untravell'd world whose margin fades
> Forever and forever when I move.

But the perpetuity of change and struggle need not be identified with the alleged inevitability of slaughter and arson. War, as practiced by man in the short span of time which history records, is neither a biological fate nor a moral law. Far from being the most shining light of life as proclaimed by the totalitarian voices of destruction, war is chaos and horror. Slavery and human sacrifices also had their apologists and priests; they also were revered as immutable features in the society of man, and were abolished at last. Blood-feuds, ordeals, and duels were proscribed by collective law; while legalized warfare itself is returning on wings, before our eyes, from standards of epic piety and chivalric honor to the indiscriminate atrocity of primal murder. These very vicissitudes of rise and degradation show that nothing eternal and holy inheres in the institution

[21]

of war. It will perish if man so wills. Whatever the misuse of a commanding ideal in the ideological verbiage of the gay 20's, the "outlawry of war" is and remains the next step in the progress of man. Peace, universal peace, is the *sine qua non* if man's advance is to be resumed beyond the present threat and ruin.

Peace, however, is not the parasitic pacifism which has eaten into our civilization and even now shelters Trojan horses and parachute columns behind the lines of our defenses. Peace at any price is peace at the price of submission. "If we mean by peace slavery," said Spinoza, "then nothing is more wretched. Peace is the harmony of strong souls, not the fightless impotence of slaves." As the price of liberty is eternal vigilance, so the price of peace is readiness to fight—the readiness that is all.

Twenty-three years ago America and the Allies fought "a war to end war." Victory and peace were wrecked by greed and fear in Europe, and by blindness in this country; but the issue remains. It contains as much of a "millennial" hope as can fructify through the effort of one generation. Whatever the well-earned failures of these last decades, "a war to end war" may be, again, the lot of our generation—and of ours alone if it rises to its task—or of others to come, until the totalitarianism of death or the universality of peace is established on earth.

Peace is indivisible. It cannot be the outcome of subtle bargaining in the clearing houses of secret diplomacy backed by standing armies; it cannot rest upon coalitions and ententes, or upon half-hearted security pacts; it cannot be achieved through structures like the League of Nations, which presumed to dispense justice without exercising power, or through one-sided and lame leaderships like that of England's and France's rulers, who neither wanted to dispense justice nor chose to exercise power. Universal peace can be founded only on the unity of man under one law and one government. Even the federated Europe of which many are still thinking is a deceptive scheme. For Europe without Britain is no Europe, it is Germany with fringes; and Europe with Britain—and with the nations of the British Commonwealth—is already the world.

Therefore the City of Man must be much more than a League of Nations or a coalescence of continents. It must be the Nation of Man embodied in the Universal State, the State of States.

The national states, indeed, built no eternal pattern of collective life. They rose from the decay of the ancient unity of Rome. They throve on the disintegration of the medieval unity of Europe. They are bound to merge again in the new unity to come.

The very speed with which so many of them have fallen in this war discloses how sick they were. It intimates that the last hour for self-sufficient national sovereignty has struck. There can be no peace for the small nations whose feeble freedom is but a gift of the stronger; there can be no peace among the giant states whose size itself bids for the anarchy of violence and conquest.

All centralizing structures—and not Germany alone, as was the fond hope of those who wagered on her early defeat—must fall into smaller federal units. All states, deflated and disciplined, must align themselves under the law of the world-state, if the world of tomorrow is to have peace.

It is universality that we oppose to totalitarianism, republican unity to autarchic despotism, service in brotherhood to regimentation in serfdom.

The one sound method for achieving peace in a world of manifold peoples and varied interests already has a long history. However hampered by the pressure of the great powers that grew around it, cantonal organization of old Switzerland actually antedates every unified national state. And the pluralistic system of the American Commonwealth, although prevented so far from reaching a complete expression—nay, even visibly weakened in this last decade by the extension of federal power—had shown in its best age that the combination of local autonomy with unitary authority is as feasible on a continental scale, and therefore ultimately on a world-wide one, as in the intimate confines of a geographically compact country.

Regional decentralization will effectually distribute power to the smallest local unit, the city and the village, down to the elemental unit which is the family, while world-wide authority will make cooperation possible among them all. These two movements—centripetal and peripheral—are essential one to the other; the first without the second would be tyranny, as the second without the first would be chaos. Together they provide a working basis for peace and freedom: an order that will be both strong and flexible without the pitiable weakness of the dwarfs and the untamable violence of the giants in our present disorder of satellites and empires.

The area of destruction must probably spread before the path is clear for the new order. And leadership with power will be necessary in the first stages of reconstruction, as long as those who have lagged behind in barbarism or inertia have not been educated to the full responsibility of their coming freedom. For democratic peace requires an effort far greater than that which enables Fascism to swamp the world with blood and mud.

But it remains for all men of good will to make the interval of preparation as short as possible, until the day comes when the heresy of nationalism is conquered and the absurd architecture of the present world is finally dismantled. Then, above the teeming, manifold life of free communities rising from the natural conditions of each one's soil and work, there will be a Universal Parliament, representing people, not states—a fundamental body of law prevailing throughout the planet in all those matters that involve interregional interests; an elected president, the President of Mankind—no crowned emperor, no hereditary king—embodying for a limited term the common authority and the common law; and a federal force ready to strike at anarchy and felony.

Diversity in unity and unity in diversity will be the symbols of federal peace in universal democracy.

Universal and total democracy is the principle of liberty and life which the dignity of man opposes to the principle of slavery and spiritual death represented by totalitarian autocracy. No other system can be proposed to the dignity of man, since democracy alone combines the fundamental characteristics of law, equality, and justice. But as there has never been a wholly Christian society in spite of the teachings of Christ and of the loyalty of some of His disciples scattered throughout the ages, so there has never been a total democracy ordering all activities of life over any great area of space and time. There were sketchy outlines of it in the ancient and medieval city-states, but they rested on foundations of slavery or serfdom. There have been closer approximations to it in the modern world, from the English revolutions of the seventeenth century to the French upheavals, and from the America of Jefferson to the America of Lincoln. But even in this country the experiment in democracy progressed only so long as formal political freedom and virtual economic equality were present together in the expanding opportunity of the open frontier.

Democracy, therefore, is an ancient hope of man

calling for fulfillment in the coming age of man. Its unity rests upon three principles. The first is universal participation in government, through the direct expression of referendum or town meeting, or through electoral mandate, or even—when the stress of the times so commands—through the delegation of all authority to a responsible chief executive freely chosen by the people for a limited term. This is the government of the people by the people, the foundation of law.

The second principle emphasizes that the state is the agent of collective human purposes, the servant of the common good, and that the demos, the unity of the people, is the permanent source of power behind those who temporarily hold it. Therefore a democracy must be always ready to rise not only against the self-appointed usurpers of power, but "against the never-ending audacity of elected persons" as well. This is the government of the people for the people, the foundation of equality.

The third principle, fundamental to the other two, establishes that a democratic community is a community of persons. Democracy, therefore, cannot be run by robots and automatons, by serfs and slaves. Its vigor rests upon the cultivation and discipline of the person, as a self-acting and self-controlling agent. Its quality is the quality of the education which it imparts to its citizens and exacts from them, in the balance of private interest and public service that makes the substance of the social contract. This is the foundation of justice.

In the decline of Western civilization the collective purpose of democracy, with its commandments of discipline and loyalty, had given way to a corrupted liberalism, with its claim of unrestricted liberty for each one to think and act as he pleased. The all-embracing benignity of this perversion reserved some applause for the rugged individualist who proved strong and free enough to kill the freedom of his countrymen; and the principle of non-interference in the domestic policies and in the mutual quarrels of other nations covered under a banner of superstitious liberalism the contraband of approval and help to whatever foreign country had freely chosen to forfeit its own freedom or had freely managed to kill the freedom of its neighbor.

Few anticipated the spread and speed of the contagion. Few realized that a world which the machine age has made much smaller than this country was in the Civil War cannot endure half free and half slave. One side must win.

What has given victory so far to the side of the enslavers in the Old World is their "secret weapon," an open secret. Unbated by mercy, envenomed by contempt, this weapon is the intransigence of their discipline, the unity of their conviction. As to the democracies, their conquerors know how weak they are, or were; for democracy, they say, "rests on opinion, it has no conviction."

A new foundation, then, must be laid for a new democracy—in the firm rock of conviction, deep below the moving sand of opinion. And the concept of a vital democracy must be dissociated from the notion of a disintegrated liberalism, which is a precursor of tyranny and a prey to it. There is, indeed, no liberty but one: the right, which is a duty, of making oneself and others free through absolute allegiance to the final goal of man. All other liberties are the rewards of battle. There is no comfort but one: pride in the duty performed. All other comforts are the ornaments of victory.

Indeed, everybody knows how sternly civil liberties were limited even in times of security and peace. No one ever thought of extending the rights of assembly and free speech to a meeting of nudists in the middle of the city or to a parliament of lepers in a public hall. No franchise of the press was recognized, no radio time was set apart, for the propaganda of theft or arson or murder, nay, not even for the publicity of free love or for direct incitements to social and economic revolt. The pillars of family and property were held unshakable and holy.

But a chorus of lamentations on the numbered days of democracy and freedom answers the request for protective measures against the "insurgent agents," the Nazis and their retinues, who are "here in the city seeking to destroy it" without even the trouble of waging a war.

Democracy, therefore, must be redefined: no longer the conflicting concourse of uncontrolled individual impulses, but a harmony subordinated to a plan; no longer a dispersive atomism, but a purposive organism. It is not a sequence of shibboleths, a pharisaic lip-service to the disembodied slogans of freedom and justice. It is the plenitude of heart-service to a highest religion embodying the essence of all higher religions. Democracy is nothing more and nothing less than humanism in theocracy and rational theocracy in universal humanism.

It is true that the value of the individual person is ultimate and that the democratic community, unlike the all-devouring totalitarian state, must be ordained to promote the welfare and fulfillment of each person. But it is equally true that no individual good life can be lived outside a good society and that the single citizen must strive toward a common good which is beyond himself as it is beyond any single community and any passing generation. Here again the centralizing and the peripheral drives are indispensable to each other.

The teachers of totalitarian philosophy have said that "everything must be within the state, nothing against the state, nothing outside the state." Democracy teaches that everything must be within humanity, nothing against humanity, nothing outside humanity. The dictatorship of humanity, on the basis of a law for the protection of human dignity, is the only rule from which we may hope for life for ourselves and resurrection for the nations that have fallen.

Definite legislation alone, however changeable in its details according to the needs of the times, and vitalized with the ever-flexible suggestions from the trial and error of the unwritten law, can describe the intricate relations of individual rights and social duties, of liberties and discipline. Nothing short of it can steer the Republic between the shoals of a self-destructive leniency and the suicidal contradiction of a fully "authoritarian democracy." But the fundamental principle is that the democratic concept of freedom can never include the freedom to destroy democracy and freedom. If no liberty is granted to the murderer and arsonist, no liberty can be granted to whosoever and whatsoever threaten the divine spirit in man and above man.

This is—in an interpretation suited to the modern mind—the spirit which Christ called the Holy Ghost. In its ultimate sacredness He set a limit to all tolerance and charity. "Wherefore I say unto you, all manner of sin and blasphemy shall be forgiven unto men: but the blasphemy against the Holy Ghost shall not be forgiven unto men."

The President of the United States has said: "Most of us, regardless of what church we belong to, believe in the spirit of the New Testament." The statement is true even for great numbers of people who are not, or never were, under the direct influence of the Scriptures. It is true even for most of those who reject all kinds of transcendent belief and cling, or think they cling, to rational knowledge and scientific experiment alone.

The universality of the New Testament, the true

catholicity of its religious vision, was first announced by Christ Himself when He added: "And whosoever speaketh a word against the Son of man"—against Christ Himself—"it shall be forgiven him: but whosoever speaketh against the Holy Ghost, it shall not be forgiven him." The religion of the Holy Ghost, and nothing else, is the "spirit of the New Testament" of which the President of the United States spoke.

This universal religion, harbored in the best minds of our age, this common prayer of democracy militant which must be the hymn of democracy triumphant, was anticipated by sages and saints of all ages. Its substance matured out of whatever rose highest in man's speculations and hopes.

The prophets of Israel contributed the Messianic promise of peace and justice on earth after long struggle, while other religious geniuses farther in Asia contemplated the final identity of man and God beyond all struggle. Greek poetry and philosophy proclaimed the perpetual validity of intellec-

tual ideas and ethical standards, and Rome strove—
largely under the influence of Stoic philosophy and
its Law of Nature—toward some kind of unitary
civilization and of equity of law. Later, the Catholic
Church asserted the brotherhood of men under the
fatherhood of God and made each soul worthy of
salvation through the harmony of God's will and
human effort which it called grace and works. The
Protestant insurrection overrode all obstacles to the
direct communication of the individual with God,
thus fundamentally asserting the freedom of man's
spirit, while—from enthusiasm for the destination
of man—humanism, the Renaissance, the revolutions, the era of liberalism rose. Finally, the optimistic philosophies of enlightenment, which provided a background for America's Declaration of
Independence, postulated the primal goodness and
nobility of man as a myth conducive to his final
nobility and goodness.

In each and all of these particular systems there
are humanity and redemption. Each and all of them

[37]

are comprehended under the all-embracing and all-interpreting religion of the Spirit.

But not even at the peak of liberal self-assurance, or at the bottom of the corruption of liberalism, has an undiscriminating freedom of worship ever been granted in the democratic world. Written and un-written laws saw to it that obscene and sanguinary cults were proscribed; even milder heresies such as Mormon polygamy were inexorably stamped out. Nothing in the record of democracy bears out the assumption that the most sacrilegious of all creeds should enjoy freedom of worship in the freedom of democracy. This creed, the Fascist-Nazi philosophy, holds as self-evident truths that men are born unequal, that they have no right to life or liberty, and that the only pursuit of happiness for the herds is on the road to slavery under the whip of self-appointed herdsmen.

The democratic freedom of worship was never valid beyond the limits of the common faith. It hardly ever extended beyond the Jewish and Christian confessions or those more unusual cults of exotic origin whose essence was akin to that of the Jewish and Christian creeds.

None of these particular creeds reached the universality of the religion of the Spirit, to which all men are witnesses. But none of them willfully and consciously conflicted with the basic tenets on which the world-religion of the Spirit is founded.

The Asiatic doctrines, to be sure, withered in a saintly inertia which made them unable—from Buddhism and earlier down to the present age—to participate decisively in struggle and progress. Tolstoyism itself, a cross of West and East, and Gandhism itself, a cross of East and West, have been unable to offset altogether the debilitating influences of Asia's passive worship and of the commandment of non-resistance to evil.

The prophetic spirit and the heroic universalism of the Hebraic tradition have been and are incessantly expressed in unorthodox and even secular forms of Jewish life. They have brought and bring a contribution of inestimable value to the spirit of democracy. But most of the Synagogue, tempted to this course no doubt by the stern problem of survival which faces the Jewish people in a hostile world, was overcome by the sterility of its unshakable conservatism and by the racial stubbornness which severed the orthodox Jew from Jesus, highest of Jewish prophets.

No apologetic is needed for the greatness of the Roman Church or for the glory of its achievement in piloting Western man through the Dark Ages. But its catholicity was severely curtailed by its constant temptation to commit the basic error of identifying the Church as a temporal kingdom with the "Kingdom of God" of Christian and prophetic expectation. This error invests the sociologically relative architecture of the Church with an unwarranted aura of unqualified holiness. An ecclesiastical institution buffeted by the vicissitudes of the centuries, conditioned by the mutation of social and political forces, subject to the corruptions which assail all institutions, claims an absoluteness of veneration which is incompatible with its relativity in history. The historical usurps the sanctity of the eternal. The consequence is particularly alarming in our day of a desperate fight between democracy and tyranny, for the Church is tempted to make peace with tyranny and come to terms with Fascism, if Fascism promises not to harm the Church as a historical institution and if those tendencies in Fascism and Nazism prevail which are prepared to pervert the Church and make it a subordinate ally of their political plans.

In former ages already Roman Christian Catholicism had often proved Roman—or French, or Spanish, or Austrian—rather than Christian and universal. In more recent years its *Syllabus of Errors* (1864), the start of a Second Counter-Reformation challenging the liberal world that had risen from Reformation and Renaissance, played into the hands of political and social obscurantism. Its spiritual totalitarianism was exploited both as a pattern and as a tool by the totalitarianism of political and social enslavement. The docility of the Church toward the powers that be and its readiness not

[41]

only to compromise but also to collaborate with evil, when collaboration is profitable, ushered in the unfortunate Lateran treaties of 1929 by which the Christian Pontificate hitched its wagon to the Fascist star.

Pious Catholics of former ages, as firm in theological belief as they were fearless in political and moral behavior, would have called today's Fascist-Catholic compact a new Babylonian captivity. But those saints and doctors who branded as a Babylonian captivity the thralldom in Avignon of the Christian Church to the French kings were more articulate than the liberal Catholics of our day.

The republic of Spain was drowned in blood, with the approval and sponsorship of the Catholic hierarchy, regardless of the hushed protests of liberal Catholics on both sides of the Atlantic. Nor had there been any stint of approval and help from the Catholic hierarchy to the burglary in Ethiopia and to the final debauchment of the League of Nations. At last, when the hour of reckoning struck, the Papacy, a voluntary prisoner in Fascism's Babylon, shrouded itself in oracular ambiguities apt to sound Fascist to Fascists and Christian to Christians, while Italian Catholic bishops blessed the flight of the Fascist vulture and hundreds of Christian bells pealed cheer in Munich, June 18, 1940, to the Führer and the Duce, meeting over the corpse of France.

Freedom-loving, justice-loving Catholics—here as well as in the Latin-American republics and wherever else they can reawaken to the examples bequeathed by braver ages—will see to it some day that humility in faith be no longer the lure to servility in politics and that allegiance to the City of God be disentangled again from bondage to Vatican City as a foreign potentate in feud or trade with other potentates.

As for the Protestant Churches, much of the vigor with which their founders had opened to man the realm of spiritual freedom was lost in hairsplitting sectarianism and theological trivialities. Most of them, moreover, have sailed without chart and compass between the Scylla of an enervating pessimism which in earlier days promised Heaven by making earth a Hell, and the Charybdis of a pointless optimism which was later borrowed from the philosophy of enlightenment. Some at least of the roots of Nazi cynicism are implicit in the Lutheran attitude of political irresponsibility and in the Lutheran glorification of the authoritarian state as the only rampart against anarchy; while, on the other hand, liberal Protestants in the democratic world joined only too zealously the decadence of the materialist and pragmatist philosophies in a creed, as delusive as it was insipid, of "prosperity around the corner." At last, when the hour of reckoning struck, and the orthodox Lutherans in Germany hastened to grovel before Hitler, the liberal Protestant Churches in the democratic world either shrank in solitary protests unheeded by the estranged masses or supported a doctrinaire pacifism willing to accept slavery and to call it peace, and watered Christian charity, which is a fighting one, down to the Quaker's entreaty to extend "love even to Hitler"—Christ's love to the Antichrist.

All this and more is true.

Yet the universal religion of the Spirit acknowledges with reverence the incorruptible substance of truth which lies under the surfaces and the errors of the separate confessions risen from the common ground of ancient and medieval civilization.

In this acknowledgment is the foundation of religious freedom in democracy.

Democracy, in the catholicity of its language, interprets and justifies the separate creeds as its own vernaculars.

It follows, then, that none of these vernaculars, however venerable and lovable, and whatever their right to citizenship, can take the place of the universal language which expresses the common belief of man. The latter explains and annexes all dogmas as symbols; the churches, in the fetters of literalism, anathematize as heresy and error the symbolical meaning that is the dogma's inmost truth. No matter how dismayed we may be by the subjugation of Europe and Asia and the ruin of more than half the civilized world, we shall not imitate the backward course of Julian the Apostate during the break-up of ancient civilization, or of the Roman populace running for asylum and atonement to old gods after the capture of their city by the Goths. We shall not turn, under the counsel of despair, from a higher and vaster religion to lesser ones.

Old cults, developed and crystallized over the centuries, will have the honorable protection of democracy; but no Church, however powerful or far-spreading, can be officially acknowledged as a religion of the state, and no Church can be granted primacy or privileges above other churches. Indeed, the desire for such a place of privilege or pre-eminence on the part of any Church would be a measure of its inadequacy to the fundamental principle of democracy. The separation of state and Church, as first provided in the Constitution of the United States, is and remains the base from which arises the supremacy of world-humanism and world-democracy—the catholicity of the common creed, which embraces and interprets every lesser faith.

This common creed already exists; toward its

[46]

luminous center all higher minds already point, from whatever distant horizon they may set out. The yoke of this creed is as easy as it is inevitable; its doctrines are as plain as they are undebatable. It teaches that a divine intention governs the universe—be it called God or Deity or the Holy Ghost or the Absolute or Logos or even Evolution. The direction of this intention is from matter to life and from life to spirit, from chaos to order, from blind strife and random impulse to conscience and moral law, from darkness to light.

It teaches that in the universe we know the human species is the spearhead of the divine intention, man the necessary ally of that "power, not ourselves, which makes for righteousness." It teaches that man's growth or progress or evolution is not backward toward the savagery of the superman or the gleam of the beast of prey, but forward toward the radiance of the angel. It teaches that if the divine intention is to be fulfilled, the pursuit of the good, under the inspiration of faith, hope, and charity, must imply resistance to evil, with battle when

[47]

necessary. It teaches that life is service, and death a gate to life—whatever the destiny of the individual person in the "undiscover'd country from whose bourn no traveller returns." For individual life is humble in the knowledge of its limits, under the all-human dogma of fallibility. It has meaning only by participation in the unlimited past, into the illimitable future; and no one man or race or generation can embody the heritage and the promise of Man.

The legacies of Greece and Palestine contribute almost equally to this creed. Passages of Plato foreshadow it. Tenets from the Lord's Prayer still sound and ever will sound adequate to it: "Thy kingdom come. Thy will be done on earth as it is in heaven."

These tenets, and the Golden Rule, and Paul's injunction, "Be ye members one of another," comprise the essential sociology and economics of democracy. "Political economy and social science," as Henry George has said, "cannot teach any lessons that are not embraced in the simple truths that were taught to poor fishermen and Jewish peasants by One who 1800 years ago was crucified."

Therefore, sophisticated shame and frivolous irony must vanish as we dare pronounce again the prayer—and now the battlecry—"Thy kingdom come." For any religion or doctrine cloaking injustice and misery on earth under the promise of some transcendent bliss to come deserves the scorn of Marx, who called them "the opium of the people."

This earth of ours is the laboratory where the validity of eternal ideas is tested under the limits of space and time. Here and now is the scene where the divine intention which governs the universe must be enforced in the field of action as it stands supreme in the heaven of the creed.

If liberty is the purpose of democracy, justice is its instrument. In the huge civil war which is rending the world, we must remember the words of an American prophet, Lincoln, against those who repulsed the dejected and the poor, who spurned the suppliants, and said or thought: "You are worthless or worse; we will neither help you nor be

[49]

helped by you. . . . . This cup of liberty which your old masters hold to your lips, we will dash from you, and leave you the chance of gathering the spilled and scattered contents in some vague and undefined when, where, and how."

We must listen again to that other American prophet, Henry George, who knew full well many years before the events where the course of inequality and injustice would lead society:

"As public spirit is lost . . . as . . . reforms become hopeless; then in the festering masses will be generated volcanic forces, which shatter and rend when seeming accident gives them vent. Strong, unscrupulous men, rising upon occasion, will become the exponents of blind popular desires or fierce popular passions, and dash aside forms that have lost their vitality. The sword will again be mightier than the pen, and in carnivals of destruction brute force and wild frenzy will alternate with the lethargy of a declining civilization."

The brute force and wild frenzy of Nazi-Fascism

are the mongrel product of rugged individualism as carried to utmost efficiency in the anarchy of *laissez-faire* liberalism, in the exploitation of the masses by competitive capitalism, and of a degenerate Socialism ("an idea misused and corrupted almost past recognition"), which substituted for the idea of justice the scheme of mass-regimentation, with its equality of servitude and its universality of deprivations.

The Führers and war-lords of our times, the conquering beasts of prey, emerged from the same ferments which had bred, at earlier stages of social decay, the colonial conquistador and the robber baron of industry, the ruthless money-maker and the political boss exploiting his municipal satrapy—or, at all stages of history, the individual felon rising against and above the community. For barbarism is not a condition that man has left behind him; when the leniency or cowardice of society shirks the daily deliberate effort which is needed to conquer the barbarism within it, the result on the local scene is the rule by gangsters and racketeers, the result on the world-scene is the rule by tyrants. Indeed, many of today's tyrants and their henchmen, before their day of glory, had been criminal offenders to whom the liberal era flung open the gates of the prisons of which they were rightful inmates.

On the other hand, the masses had been cowed to serfdom through bleak decades of training in the impotence of class-struggle and class-grudge and through the fading of all faith and hope except the crude dogma of materialism and the desire for rising standards of living and steadier security. This and more was their due—nor is the guilt of monopolistic capitalism redeemed by the error of the misled masses; but the Führers and enslavers can endorse some of these promises: if not of plenty, of equality in misery and of security in the dusk of the manger. Small wonder that Hitler boasts to be "not only the destroyer, but the executor of Marx." For he really has stripped Marxism of what was good and human in it and has put into effect all the evil in it. Stalin, working through from the other end, inevitably reaches Hitler, in the middle of the same darkness.

[52]

The compact of Marxist Russia with Nazi Germany, August 1939, was no less ominous than the agreement between the Roman Church and Fascist Italy had been ten years earlier. But Marx himself, the prophet of the poor, had missed the higher implications of his prophecy and burdened his hope with a load of hatred and of materialistic error. Nor, for all his moral genius and intellectual scope, could he step beyond the mental boundaries of that very bourgeoisie which he so vehemently loathed. Bourgeois, nay, reactionary, ideas were those, so dear to him, of class, of insurrection, of dictatorship; bourgeois was the shape of his Commune, a colossal capital city in the flare of revolt; bourgeois was the ordinance of his proletariat, a standing army of Napoleonic origin with the general strike or immobilization as the imitative counterpart to military mobilization; bourgeois, finally, with the pernicious expansion of bourgeois technology toward the infinity of power, was his scheme of the labor-state: one colossal factory, pressing under iron ceilings the breath and the sweat of millions. At last Lenin came and said: "Every large machine-industry—which is the material productive source and the basis of Socialism—requires an absolute and strict unity of the will. . . . But how can we secure a strict unity of the will? *By subjecting the will of thousands to the will of one."*

Now men were herds, panic-stricken and ready for the wolves. The Blitzkrieg, the battles of Flanders and France, had the flashing speed of an inescapable epilogue. The victors bartered their quality of human beings for the drunkenness of primacy and the exultation of rapine. The vanquished, caught—not so much in strategic pincers as in the double despair of capitalistic oppression and communistic snare—dissolved in disaster, to relax finally in the benumbed felicity of a subhuman bondage.

They all, victors and vanquished, will be slaves unless they rise again, unless we lend our hand that they may rise again. If they do not, they all will be the vanguard of pitiable generations groveling, back over the crossroads of nature, to the elementary economy and the animal automatism of bee-hive and ant-hill. They themselves will know that even the vaunted security which their tyrants promise as a safeguard against unemployment and class-struggle cannot conceal for long the ugliness of its real picture: a barren livelihood bordering on famine and squalor. The hours of labor will grow at the crack of their slave-holders' whip while the productivity of the soil and of the engine will slacken at the touch of uninspired hands. For prosperity is the fruit of ingenuity, and ingenuity blossoms only on the branch of freedom.

Ere all comfort and plenty, all pleasure and joy, become to the children of man nothing but dim reminiscences of a fabulous past, we want to champion again—in the fullness of its splendor and in the wholeness of its feasibility—the human dream, the American dream. This dream is not the dream of capitalism, which made of Freedom the murderer of Equality, nor of Communism, which made of Equality the strangler of Freedom. Neither is it the scheme of a resurgent feudalism, or corporative economy, which promises peace and order in the compulsory fixity of everyone wherever birth or chance happened to place him. For there is no gainsaying that technical assets are in some of the plans for syndical trade unions and associations of professions and crafts; but corporations and guilds, as advocated by clerical and political groups of the Right, are pious nicknames of Fascism, lures for weary men anxious to be freed from freedom.

A new trail must be blazed. It must be run to its ultimate end.

All the children of the earth must know that they all have inherited the earth. There must be no place any longer for those who own and do not work above and against those who work and do not own. Man, recovering from his guilty blindness, must become aware at last that the problem of production, which was a problem of power, has been virtually superseded by the problem of distribution, which is a problem of justice. For the earth, fertilized by a science which man, its author, has long failed to master, can become mature for a golden age, generous to billions.

Economy can be pluralistic and flexible, with its primary centers transferred from the metropolitan

cities to the villages, close to the friendlier suggestions of nature. Federal aggregations—each of them
dedicated to a specialized purpose, of sport or industry, of education or art, of administration or
trade—could collect around focal points the energies
radiating from the smaller communities.

The factory, in whose self-contained despotism
Fascism found an early blueprint of world-wide
regimentation, must be no longer the penitentiary of
the outcast, the Bastille of the proletariat. In a more
human world it should take the place which is held
by the military barracks in our pre-human era. The
youth of the nations, enlisted for a limited term,
should learn in federal factories, in public works, on
communal farms, the skill of production in patience
rather than the craft of destruction in terror. The
machine will forge wings, not chains. Slavery will
be anathema, and partnership the rallying cry. The
distribution of service, assigning to each one his
share of labor and leisure, must make of unemployment—with its restlessness fermenting to revolt—a
forgotten nightmare.

Private property will be admitted as biologically

inevitable and socially useful. But the Bill of Rights pledging that no private property shall be "taken for public use without just compensation" must be supplemented with a Bill of Duties stating that no private property can be tolerated outside the framework of just social use. Limits must be thus set to the accumulation of wealth and to its transmission down the generations.

Morals will have the primacy over economics, not economics over morals. Injustice, ever recurrent in the vicissitudes of human progress, must be fought as soon as it rears its head. No quarter must be given to the paradox of moral man in immoral society, or of poverty in the midst of plenty. Bread must know no fear. Love and parenthood must unlearn fear and shame.

Yes, beyond the black age we raise the flag of God's kingdom on earth.

There is an Old Testament of Americanism. It incorporates the words and deeds of the American endeavor, from the Declaration of Independence to the plea by Woodrow Wilson for the League of Nations before the Senate Committee on August 19, 1919. There must be a New Testament of Americanism, which will voice the commandments that have arisen from this age of denial and ruin, from America's desertion of the League of Nations to the cataclysm of 1940.

The word of early Americanism was "separation." The Commonwealth, proud of its republican Constitution, confident of its future, seceded from feudalism and privilege, from arbitrary power and caste distinctions, such as still prevailed overseas during America's formative years. This New World of ours stood for a clean slate and a fresh start, and the word "separation" retained a creative meaning as long as the young nation—in the era of the nations—was allowed to grow and mature, unhampered by the tutelage of the motherland.

Then separation was degraded into the doctrine of isolation: a word of self-destruction. It rallied the defeaters of Wilson, who defeated themselves and their people in the delusion of seclusion and autarchy, of unchangeable separation in a changing world. The era of the nations was over. A supranational world was rising already from the ruins of the first World War. The machine was contracting the oceans and telescoping the distances. And the very size of America makes her unfit to hide. No Byzantine or Chinese wall can protect the Western Hemisphere. If the United States clings to separation she must fall: nothing more than another colony collapsing with the downfall of the home countries.

Thus, the New Testament of Americanism must identify itself with World Humanism. "Separation" must be replaced with "unity," Independence must be integrated into Interdependence. The "injuries and usurpations" of the minor tyrants from whom the Declarants of Independence cut themselves loose had "in direct object the establishment of an absolute Tyranny over these States." But the monarchs of today have in direct object the establishment of an absolute tyranny over all the states of the world. The Prussia of 1917 could already be envisaged by Wilson as "a challenge to all mankind." But the world-conqueror of today is actually the man who threatens all other men.

Therefore all that survives of mankind must breathe in one breath and fight in one fight, since the whole earth has become one living-space or dying-space for all nations of men. We cannot divide the world with Fascism, which is, by definition, totalitarian. We can have no freedom or safety for ourselves unless we are ready to reclaim the world from Fascism, to win the world for a new order— unless we endow democracy with a fighting spirit, and meanwhile hold the fort until the day comes when Goliath meets his David.

Nothing could be more shocking to America's humility and pride than the necessity to take leadership among the nations. Much of the charm and fluency of her life, much of her self-assured detachment, will be gone. And yet no necessity is more imperative. For the nations have fallen from the tree of Europe, shaken by their own disloyalty, and the one that still holds, however splendid in her struggle and sacrifice, can hardly be expected to resume a world-inspiring mission until help and rescue, with renovation and unity, come from the strongest of her offspring. England, too, had declined in appeasement and surrender; the vigor of her democracy, too, had slackened under the monopoly of ruling cliques and the delusion of national egoism. A juster social order has been promised by the British Labor Party to a victorious Britain, but no self-sufficient British victory—and no rule by Labor—is in sight. Union was proposed by the British Government to France, later than at the eleventh hour. But the offer, futile in the death-agony of republican France, remains a mere ideal milestone on the slow path of man toward the consciousness that the era of the nations is over and that unity will be achieved in the spirit of Evil if the spirit of Good is not good enough. No union was possible between England's will to resist and France's will to succumb. And no final union now

[62]

is feasible among the states that still call themselves democracies, until the spirit of democracy is heightened again to moral fervor and social charity within the boundaries of each one of those who will be called to be the charter members of world-union tomorrow.

Thus, while England endures and bleeds—and must of necessity postpone to an indefinite future definite plans for what must follow the war—no one is left free and strong enough to show the way toward social reform and universal order except this country. Its failures—both in intellect and in action, in education and in politics—must be bared remorselessly to its knowledge of self. But the knowledge of error must be the alarm to its ancient virtues, that they, fully awake again, may raise America to the dignity and power of her inevitable mission.

For inevitable it is. Wilson, on the eve of the declaration of war to the Germany of his time, said: "We are but one of the champions of the rights of mankind." But we may be forced soon to say: "We

are the one champion of the rights of mankind."
Inevitably already, England and the English-
speaking nations are calling on this country to
"join hands" for help and leadership. This is but
the preliminary to a greater and more burdensome
task.

Leadership, to be sure, implies some sort of imperium. But there is a difference between imperial-
ism and imperium, between those whom their own
lust for power chooses for a self-appointed primacy
which is the right of might and those who are
chosen by the objective circumstances of history
for a privilege which is a service, for a right which
is a duty. This is, indeed, the substance of a chosen
people: power in the frame of service.

We have been reminded recently of Bacon's
saying: "Rome did not spread upon the world; the
world spread upon the Romans." This was the
destiny of other nations and cultures, in ancient and
in modern ages as well. This—to the largest extent
of world-leadership for world-communion in the
comradeship of man—is the destiny of America, as

[64]

manifest as it was unwanted, since the English-speaking nations were "left to fight alone," and all the world must sink unless we take the helm.

For rulership by the strongest and wisest is the prescribed path to the equality of all, if the strong can learn wisdom and if rulership is accepted in the spirit of reluctance and devotion that Plato suggests to all rulers. There are in the family of nations children who must grow up, sick who must be cured, maniacs who must be confined, criminals who must be apprehended, before maturity and redemption become the common lot. The healing of the world requires a firm hand. But this hand must refrain from anything which might substantiate in any way the battlecry of the self-styled "proletarian nations" against the "starvers" of the world, "the holders of territories," the "pluto-democracies" clinging "to all the riches and gold on earth." The final goal can never be forgotten. Justice, which is the common good, can never be perverted into the interest of the stronger.

American leadership is world-trusteeship; the

Pax Americana a preamble to the *Pax Humana*.

We, the signers of this statement, have here declared the faith which unites us and the hope which we share. This faith and hope need not be discouraged by the smallness of our number and the limitations of our power. For we remember that the destructive upheaval which is now shaking the earth started from humbler origins in conventicles of lost souls in Milan and in Munich some twenty years ago. They had stumbled upon the deeper pathological yearnings of the time. But we know that Good, if it is purposeful, must prove stronger at last than the fundamental instability of Evil.

Purpose, therefore, creative and expansive purpose, must be given to the democratic world with an affirmative and missionary will replacing its passive defenses of today. Readiness to criticize the old rather than to build up systematically the new, propensity to oppose rather than to propose, made the original weakness of the Protestant world. We for our own part shall perish, if nothing is on our side but the spirit of negation and protest implicit in the very words Antifascism and Antinazism. Democracy, no longer a retreating antagonist, must claim a protagonist's role. The emergency of democracy must be the emergence of democracy.

No spirit of revolution animates our proposals, since revolution, an obsessive myth of the modern mind in its decay, is but the counterpart of war. It is war itself, with fire and steel, with fraud and terror; nor is there any comforting choice between perpetual revolution as projected by extreme Communism into the infinity of Evil and eternal war as hallowed by Fascism and Nazism in their black masses.

We do not think that an overthrow is requisite or that blood must run and flame must burn on new deceitful altars. We do think that America is strong and flexible enough to grow up, the equal of her promise, and to live up to herself—in a reformation of the Reformation, in a discipline of liberty, in a restatement of Democracy. Democracy and the Constitution will interpret themselves, in the inspiration of the changing age. And the new tenets of Americanism will be to its ancient prophecies what the New Testament was to the Old.

It did not come to destroy the law or the prophets, but to fulfill them. "For verily . . . one jot or one tittle shall in no wise pass from the law, till all be fulfilled."

The Premier of England has said: "We are moving through a period of extreme danger and of splendid hope." America will not shrink from being the standard-bearer of the splendid hope.

Patriotic vanity alone could blind her eyes to the blemishes that endanger the fulfillment of her tasks: the degraded education, the corrupted political machines, the efficiency of the dollar-hunter, the inertia of the forgotten man. But defeatism alone could make her unaware of the signs that are contained both in her heritage from the past and in the perseverance of her hope for the future.

It is good that this country was never allowed to be the exclusive fief of any single stock, not even that English stock whose language we proudly speak and whose tradition we faithfully share. It is manifest destiny that representatives came here from all races and regions—from Europe and Africa, from Asia and Polynesia—thus lifting the young nation above the level of the old and molding the New World into a scheme of the All-World to come.

The Jew among us, survivor of persecutions, warns us by his very presence that anti-Semitism is the entering wedge of racism, the dusk of hatred which precedes the totalitarian night. The Negro himself, with whom our failure was most inglorious, helps us by reminding us that our slow progress is a mere token of the justice we pledged—until all races rise to equality in maturity.

Nineteen centuries ago it was said: "There is neither Greek nor Jew nor Barbarian nor Scythian." The promise was taken up and expanded in the universality of the American creed. "There is neither Jew nor Gentile, neither native nor naturalized, neither master nor slave, neither white nor colored." It was often betrayed but never withdrawn. The American creed must be the American deed.

It is good, although tragic, that we may "be left to fight alone." For all false pretenses have fallen, and distance and delay do not cloud our sight any longer. Good, although tragic, it is that the prayers of the appeasers of Europe were not granted, and that, them notwithstanding, the world has been "divided into two opposite ideological camps."

One of these camps is where we stand. This country is now more than a structure of ground and water, of mountains and plains. It is and must be the shrine of whatever is human, the ark of life.

Here, and here alone, the continuity of ancient and modern wisdom lives in a Constitution which, needful though it may be of partial improvements and technical changes, has blended in exemplary manner through several generations the unity of leadership symbolized by presidential authority with the substance of aristocracy represented by specialized skill, and with popular suffrage, which

[70]

is the mainstay of democracy. Here—more precious than all the gold in Kentucky—the treasure of English culture is guarded, as Hellenism was preserved in Rome; and along with it the treasure and essence of all human cultures. Here, and almost nowhere else, is Europe: the Europe-America that will become "all things to all men" to "save them all." For here, and almost nowhere else, is man granted the right and duty of being Christian and human.

No one, indeed, is an American by birthright alone, and the man who is only an American is not yet an American. But all those are Americans who pledge their lives, their fortunes, and their sacred honor to the creed of universal democracy in the expectation of a world-society for men united to fight their common enemies, the untamed forces of Fate and Evil. Whether they claim an ancestry of centuries or whether they themselves landed from Mayflowers of hope and will, they all call fatherlands the distant lands whence they or their ancestors fled from injustice and bondage. Of this country they know that its intimate name is Philadelphia, the City of Brotherly Love. They know that of it, and of all fading fatherlands, one Brotherland will be made, the City of Man; and that the United States must be the Uniting States. No number is prescribed to the stars on its flag.

We, the signers of this statement, coming as we do from various lands and contrasting backgrounds, nevertheless have experienced already in our group how the community of the peril that confronts the world and us voids the individual differences and gives to our deliberations a unity which we hardly hoped for. In this consensus we find, with all due humility, a pledge for a more comprehensive unity among all men of good will.

Therefore we address our words to those from Plymouth Rock and to those from Ellis Island, for to both alike, Americans old and new, shines "the lamp beside the golden door." We address them to the American youth, whatever the differences of racial origins and social status among them. They all, ere it is too late, will reject the guidance of a

[72]

false education, the teachings of a degraded science, the sophistry of the irresponsibles. It is through them that all America will be youth, to rejuvenate the world. Theirs is the task, and theirs is the honor, of bringing, across the darkness, "man's solar period" to its new beginning.

October 31, 1940

Herbert Agar

Frank Aydelotte

G. A. Borgese

Hermann Broch

Van Wyck Brooks

Ada L. Comstock

William Yandell Elliott

Dorothy Canfield Fisher

Christian Gauss

Oscar Jászi

Alvin Johnson

Hans Kohn

Thomas Mann

Lewis Mumford

William Allan Neilson

Reinhold Niebuhr

Gaetano Salvemini

Proposal

"It was the fundamental error of the jurists and law-makers to think they could create life by means of a constitution and a code of laws. . . . Constitutions can only conclude real developments; they can never precede them. Artificial construction violates life." This is the Fascist philosophy of chaos in words ascribed to Hitler. "The pursuit of the random path of intelligence," he added, "was the real defection of man from his divine mission."

Intelligence, that is the divine in man, must accept the challenge. Its record in the creation of life stretches from the sages of Greece and the law-givers of Israel to the Fathers of the American Constitution. Its will and purpose must rise anew against the blindness of instinct and the fury of perpetual revolution.

We believe that the endeavors of Plato and of his successors to outline a good Republic, a vital and durable society of men, must be resumed by men of today. We also believe that the dangers of Utopian speculation can be avoided by a collective effort, enlightened by mutual criticism and help, and that the intellectual rigor which we must borrow from the ancient tradition of culture can acquire flexibility through alloy with the factual experimentalism in which the English-speaking nations always excelled.

Society may be likened to a triangular pyramid with its three faces representing the constitutional order, the economic order, the international order. None of them stands alone; each of them leans on the others. All three together converge toward the common apex, which is the freedom and dignity of human personality. All three rise together from the common base, which is the moral belief and the religious faith of the community.

We therefore have agreed that four groups of experts should be appointed, under the guidance of a central committee, to study the four leading issues of American and world democracy. Definite proposals should be formulated at the end of a limited time and submitted to the public under the collective responsibility of the committee and of its staff.

1

The first of the four issues concerns the relations between democracy, or government by the people for the people, and individual liberties. It calls for a systematic description of freedom under a constitutional order so that the citizen may be protected not only against the threat of the external tyrant but against the treason of his fellow-citizen as well. Lincoln, in his final address, said that "important principles may and must be inflexible," but the hour has struck when such "inflexible principles" must be precisely stated in a renovated law, beyond which freedom is felony.

This, among the faces of the pyramid which symbolizes the structure of democracy, is the most patently exposed to the attack of Fascism. "We shall always be stronger than the democracies," Hitler is reported to have said, "in being able to guide their public opinion according to our wish. They cannot defend themselves against such attacks, for otherwise they would have to become authoritarian themselves. This creates such an inequality that even considerable differences in military strength are neutralized by it." While accepting the challenge, we must learn what is vital in the lesson.

Liberty, indeed, if it is not to offer a "more or less decomposed corpse" for conquerors or Quislings to tread down, must implement the promises of the Bill of Rights with the commandments of a Bill of Duties. The "enlightened self-interest" of pragmatic and utilitarian liberalism must fall in line with co-operation and service. A higher law than the will of a single and momentary majority—

which by a single act might destroy democracy itself—was always recognized, whether written or not, by democracy in its creative periods. It protected the rights of future majorities against the landslide of passing emotions and the vicissitudes of ephemeral interests. This law, a law of permanence, must be restored—and written.

Much of constitutional democracy no doubt will and must remain unwritten. No separation of powers, no checks and balances, no judicial guardianship can be substituted for the inner restraint of self-imposed tolerance and of devotion to human personality. The right to dissent must ever be upheld as the mainstay of democracy. Margins as wide as possible must be left to the fluidity of interpretation and change, to experiment even in doubtful ventures, if the spirit of democracy, which is perennial adolescence and growth, is not to calcify in the literalism of the written codes. On the other hand, a constitution of democracy cannot remain any longer negative only—a mere outline of the limits prescribed by self-restraint and tolerance, a Palladium of freedom without the armor of discipline. If American democracy is to live and become the pattern of a world to come, a constitutional reform is needed, both in the field of liberty and duty and in the relations between legislative and executive power.

The crisis of civil liberties in these fateful years has shown, and will show more definitely in the near future, how urgent is a redefinition of their meaning and scope. No less cogent is the evidence that the deterioration of parliamentarism has helped to wreck the democracies of Europe and saps our own. The compulsions of survival and of social security dictate the necessity for strengthened executive authority within a stricter frame of responsibility before the electorate and the commonwealth, since responsibility, severed from this authority to act with power, and atomized among too many, becomes elusive or vanishes altogether. As soon as the representative system, grown obtrusive and riotous, glories in crippling the executive, democracy itself is castrated and paralyzed.

On the other hand, as soon as power is given by democracy to the executive enabling it to arrive at decisions of public interest and to overcome "the law's delay," democracy is confronted with the opposite threat of the "insolence of office." If the judiciary must abdicate some of its inhibitive censorship on innovation and speed, the electorate in turn must be provided with guarantees effective enough to hold in check the whims and usurpations of elected persons. These are new conflicts arising from new situations. They cannot be solved by evading them along the functional lines of a corporate state or by increasing still further the backstage play of pressure groups. To such conflicts, and to the possibility of mediating them in the structural harmony of a more sincere legislation, we call the attention of our colleagues and friends. The emergency of democracy must be the emergence of democracy.

It is true that the high temperature of war may weld vital democracies and bring back a renewed feeling of partnership. For years to come, our fight for survival will of necessity foster this democratic brotherhood of sacrifice —if we are brothers enough to survive. But that brotherhood must survive even victory. The primary groups of family, educational association, neighborhood, and church —each of them with its specific attributes and all of them with their combined contributions to the general purpose—must be restored in new forms with new life. This is tantamount to stating that a constitutional reform of democracy cannot be founded but on the spirit of a new religion.

2

The second issue, therefore—to whose basic quality we are immediately referred from our first approach to the most visible aspect of the democratic crisis—contemplates the relations between the community as a whole and the separate churches. It asks for definite tenets embodying the universal religion of Democracy, which shall underlie each and all of them. For virtually all of them have meddled in the anarchy of the nations and bowed to the powers that be. Lincoln already had noticed that "each invokes God's aid against the others" so that "the prayers of both could not be answered." But not yet at that time had a Hitler thanked, "in humility, God for His blessings" amidst the peals of Germany's Christian bells celebrating through seven days the triumphs of an Antichrist. Therefore the hour has struck when we must know what limits are set by the religion of freedom, which is democracy, to the freedom of worship, and of what God we talk when we repeat, from the Gettysburg Address, that "this nation," and with this nation the world, "must have a new birth of freedom *under God.*"

In broad terms the task here is to determine what religious and ethical traditions are of greater or lesser value for the preservation and growth of the democratic principle. This task is obviously one which cannot be fulfilled by amateurish attempts to emulsify in sentimental combinations the contrasting religions without any one of them forgoing any one of its claims or even so much as dulling the edge of its inherent dogmatic intolerance. The attempt which we propose is of another kind—not toward confusion but toward clarification. An inquiry into the religious heritage of the Western world should try to discover which of its elements are more apt to co-operate with the democratic community and consequently more deserving of protection and help by it, and whether other elements, conversely, are by their nature and content so committed to the support of Fascist and other autocratic philosophies and intrinsically so inimical to democracy, or at least so ambiguous, as to become a source of additional danger in the hour of peril. Such an inquiry also should help to disclose whether and in how far religious and ethical traditions which emphasize freedom and the rights of the individual may obscure or neglect the collective duties and responsibilities which democratic communities must assume. It should likewise make clear whether and to what extent perfectionist principles in religious faiths and cults, while helpful in detecting the relative evils and errors of specific historic conclusions, may enervate the will to defend and to extend relative justice, and bring confusion into the choices between greater and lesser evils which constitute the alternatives of all collective decisions.

The results of analyses of this kind would determine the attitudes of the sovereign democratic society toward the particular religious associations within it. That Nazism, like any other species of totalitarian nationalism, has tried to annihilate or at least humiliate all religious communities is a tribute to their virtue as bearers of supra-temporal and supra-national loyalties. But if such loyalties are not expressed and organized in the frame of uncompromising devotion to the universality of God and man, the confessions and churches within the nation are only too liable to succumb to enslavement by the state and to hire themselves for despotic purposes. This is the pitfall of Protestant sects. On the other hand, if the supra-national loyalties are expressed and organized in political terms, the members of a supra-national church may prove equally prone, although for different motives, to become the tools of political plans inimical to democracy and claiming universal validity while actually serving very special interests. This is the danger of Roman Catholicism. The Communist International, with its questionable relations to Russian foreign policy, is a secularized version of a supra-national religion with political commitments. In some of its ways it acts as an heir to the Eastern or old Tsarist church.

The problem admits of no easy solution. Its juridical and constitutional alternatives are heavily strained between the opposite risks of democracy's forfeiting its freedom of worship and of democracy's inviting treason—more effective when cloaked with piety and justified by faith. Yet the difficulties themselves testify to the gravity of the problem and to its compelling timeliness. Already the blundering and bungling of democracy whenever a new sect, like Jehovah's Witnesses, steps unexpectedly to the fore, or its helplessness whenever an older religion wins a degree of influence beyond the limits to which the era of pragmatic liberalism had been comfortably accustomed, is token enough of a situation which bids for a vigorous, however judicious, revision of habits and laws. To be sure, separation of state and church must remain the premise of the democratic law on religions. But separation, in this field too, was degraded to isolationism or pretended aloofness and willful ignorance. Its consequences are increasingly visible in practices of unctuous collusion and mutual bribery between state and churches. In this field too, as in the general field of civil liberties in constitutional order, the sovereignty of the democratic community must stand above the liberty of each particular group, and the negative outline of the limits prescribed by self-restraint and liberal tolerance must be filled with positive knowledge and criticism—or even permit intervention when the latter becomes the lesser evil.

The same group of experts entrusted with the study of the issue of religion should explore the conflicts and solutions in the issue of education. The two are at bottom one and the same, since, as was authoritatively stated, "education in Western democracy has been the substitute for a national—and supra-national—religion." Here too the problem is to preserve the advantages of unhampered opinion and research while preventing the freedom of learning from being used as a cover for the evil-doings of the "historic relativism" and the "healthy skepticism" that have made our generations lose their way. The pruning of this tree of freedom will not make it less fruitful. The organization of learning, with colleges and universities at the top of its structure, has built and builds the preparatory ground where democratic aristocracies are trained for leadership. But no aristocracy or leadership can subsist without a firm footing in inflexible principles and unshakable values. A reorientation of education and a supervision of its aims should be undertaken from this angle.

It will not be forgotten, however, that the educational system of the Western democracies has been and still is, in spite of its shortcomings, the most conspicuous asset for the maintenance of our civilization. The obstacles to creative endeavor have been of the obstructive rather than of the destructive sort. Colleges and universities have even developed, almost spontaneously, in their chapel services and exercises a provisional model for an unsectarian liturgy—virtually adequate to a new religion outside the literal fences of each separate faith and embracing the spiritual substance of all.

3

The third issue points to the need of a profound economic reform outlining in detail the law of the common wealth, the era of distributive justice. For there cannot be any birth or rebirth of freedom under God unless it be a God of justice, manifest in breath and bread, beyond and above the vicious era which saw monopolistic capitalism and materialistic communism concurrently lift to the dignity of supreme virtues the three capital sins of greed, pride, and envy. Therefore the Declaration of Independence shall be upheld not only in so far as it states each man's inalienable rights to life and liberty and the pursuit of happiness, but in the final oath as well, which consecrates to a common duty beyond each individual's rights "our lives, our fortunes" and pledges to this duty "our sacred honor."

The need for opening to man's hope a new course, different both from the capitalism of big business and from the Communism of Marx and of the Soviet state, has been stressed only too often; but no such course has been so far recognizably charted. Discoverers in economics like Thorstein Veblen, or legislators and prophets like Henry George, usually have been overlooked by the public mind, either sated in the routine observance of a classic liberalism far from adjusted to the new standards of production and consumption, or swept by passionate proselytism or hostility toward the restless scheming of European revolutionary schools. The time seems ripe for competent students of economic history and theory, free from bigotry

and prejudice, to examine the nature of our social disorder, with their attention bent on articulate projects
designed to secure as much of stability and collective prosperity as may be attained in an age of reconstruction after
the present ruin.

This field, no doubt, is that in which the requirements
of technical precision and positive control are most exact-
ing, since economic life has a bodily weight which anchors
to the ground of immediate verifiable fact the inventions
of the mind. In this field, therefore, even less than in
any other can specific results be anticipated from a general
proposal, and it is easily admissible that some of the more
definite plans of reform as sketched in the foregoing
Declaration are subject on further inquiry to interpretation and change. The main directions, however, may be
pointed out as follows:

Projects of political and ethical interference in economic
life remain Utopian unless they are in agreement with the
interests of groups strong enough to enforce their ideal
premises. So far we must accept the materialistic point of
view. But, beyond this initial coincidence, such premises
or principles act far more powerfully than as mere labels
for material interests, and they acquire a dynamic power
of their own. Marxism would hardly have gripped the
masses if its economic motivation had not been im-
plemented with the resources of a moral will to justice.

In the same way, Washington's and Lincoln's wars would have collapsed in defeat at their very outbreak if Washington had cared for little more than the abolition of the tea-tax and Lincoln had fought as the *condottiere* of New England industrialism. This means that an economic reform must start from the twofold foundation of technical necessity and of moral, or religious, purpose. A real *Realpolitik* is applied ethics.

A return to slavery—in a modern version of it, more thoroughgoing and widespread than history has ever known before—is the general trend of this age. The origins of the evil are both moral and economic, and so must be the treatment. From the economic point of view, the workman is bought by the totalitarian state for a minimum of sustenance and security, the counterpart of which is the loss of everything else, and first of all of liberty. Vocational choice, the right to quit employment, the right of fair hearing, are eliminated, and it is the employer alone who assigns the kind of labor, who fixes the duration of employment, who administers "justice," and inflicts punishment. The employer, in turn, is shown by ultimate analysis to be none other than the state. Substantial residues of profit are conceded by it—in Fascism and Nazism and perhaps already again, albeit in disguise, by totalitarian Communism—to half-privileged groups, as connecting links between the past and the future, or between autocracy and the mob. But the concession is revocable without notice, and ownership is a sham as free enterprise is a remembrance. Neither in upper nor in lower social strata is there any room left for the "forgotten man," since the state and its police keep accurate record of each and everyone. This economy of servitude and waste, climaxing in production as armament and in war as loot, is misnamed "planned economy."

The planned economy which is implicit in the spirit of democracy is of a different sort. The ideal goal here is to make bread and shelter as freely accessible to everybody as water, the use of roads, and a number of public services now are in areas of advanced civilization. In more realistic terms, the problem is to make everybody sure of a decent minimum of sustenance, without the counterpart of slavery enforced by courts-martial, and with the discipline of social service so distributed as to prevent a feeling of earned security from degenerating into the malcontent idleness of parasitical relief. If in the field of constitutional order the trend of a reformed democracy must be restrictive, tying the Bill of Rights to a Bill of Duties, in the economic field, conversely, it must be expansive, supplementing the Bill of Political Rights with a Bill of Economic Rights. Results of this kind can be approximated along a flexible line of compromise, since compromise— not necessarily a foul one—is in the very nature of democ-

[89]

racy. There is no point in assailing, violently though but verbally, capitalism as merely the villain and in refurbishing the quaint battlecry, "Property is theft"; for capitalism, the outcome of an earnest and toilsome historical process, is not wiped out with posters and slogans. Nor is there any point in excommunicating Socialism, for Socialism, or whatever other name may denote some form of collectivism and socialized democracy, is with us to stay, whether one likes it or not.

They are, indeed, the Janus faces of democracy, mutually conditioned. From its principle of freedom democracy looks toward capitalism, which it envisions as natural, even if not unqualifiedly necessary; while from its principle of justice democracy looks toward collectivism, which it considers as necessary, even if not so conformant to nature. The balance between the two principles could be maintained as long as profit economy and consumers'-need economy were one and the same. It broke when these two economies went asunder. This, in turn, was partly due to moral deterioration in both the spheres of production and of consumption as in both the categories of employers and of employees; while, in a sequence of stricter economic forces, it was largely the blind effect of the immaturity and overgrowth of the machine age. This substituted mass production, often unnecessary and intrinsically vicious, for differentiated craftsmanship. It cast on the workman's hours the pall of passive drill, subduing the diligence of the human person serving the machine to the automatic beat of the machine itself. Together with concomitant causes and especially with the sudden dislocations of world-output and world-markets, it exposed both capital and labor to the threat and panic of idleness, as profit dwindled and unemployment simultaneously increased. Crisis followed crisis at shortening intervals, until they merged in one—of universal size and chronic duration.

Yet, the perturbations of this greatest of all technological revolutions—like those of the early ages of metallurgy and trade, as adumbrated in lurid myths by the shocked memory of antiquity—must be regarded as the clouded dawn of a better day. If the machine, man's creature, seems to have developed a brutal power of its own, there abides in the human mind a presentiment that it can and must be domesticated somehow. A further advance in mechanical ingenuity together with a change in man's purpose should provide the setup for a new extensive economy to replace in large measure the intensive one under which our world falters. It does not seem likely so far that the full benefits of technology can be reaped without rebuilding our big cities, but the possibility is already conceivable of stimulating with autonomous power minor and even minimal branches for renovated forms of home industry and individual artisanship. The centrifugal trend from urban conglomerations is a sign of the future; while production for use instead of for financial returns is abundantly exemplified in public works and institutions of welfare and learning, pointing to a society not wholly expressed in terms of money. Such signs and trends must and can be interpreted and activated; co-operatives, whose early achievements in pre-Nazi Scandinavia and in pre-Fascist Italy bore implications of world-wide import, can and must be promoted and multiplied, as bridges across the gap between producers' and consumers' economy. But, whatever particular schemes may be devised by economists and social philosophers responsive to the objective suggestions of a changing world, one general inspiration will be behind them. Fascist totalitarianism, sprung from the diseases of a disintegrating democracy, has forced the two divergent tensions of the democratic spirit—of freedom toward capitalism, of justice toward collectivism—into one circular unity, the strangling ring of National Socialism. This calamitous circle, of Capitalism-Communism as enemy brothers or as mutual accomplices, must be broken, and the two components of democracy—economic freedom and economic justice—must be reconciled in associative and complementary work for an age of creative splendor in which neither the individual's rights emerge into anarchy nor his duties submerge him in slavery.

Much reliance should be put on the genius for selective

and inventive social adjustments which marks the experience of the English-speaking nations, in their ability, tireless so far, to build, as it were, firm pile-dwellings amidst the turbulent waters of historic change. Of all essays for the economic remolding of democracy, the most important to date has been the New Deal. Its failures, like the NRA, have been largely due to an empirical groping not sufficiently illuminated by a consistent philosophy. Its achievements, in endeavors like the TVA, the NYA, and others, survive both the murmurs of the Left, which suspects them as stratagems of an undefeated capitalism, and the resentment of the Right, which brands them as Communism in thin disguise. More relevant, however, than its specific merits and flaws is the general value of its experiment in introducing a nucleus of planned economy into the loosened texture of free enterprise; and, whatever its fortunes in an immediate future, its intention will remain directive in an era of evolutionary growth. For evolution, not revolution, is the hope and will of creative democracy.

4

The fourth issue, finally, calls for a definite law of international, or supra-national order, and sovereignty of mankind. Wilson, the last prophet in the Old Testament of Americanism, said: "We are at the beginning of an age in which it will be insisted that the same standards of conduct and of responsibility for wrong done shall be observed among the nations and their governments that are observed among the individual citizens of civilized states." It follows, then, that spontaneous observance of such standards in supra-national relations cannot be expected of groups and nations who do not respect them within their own boundaries, and that no plan of universal order can be detached from the relative degree of civilization attained by those who are to partake in it.

Therefore, the prerequisites for any world-structure that can be designed today are constitutional order, ethico-religious purpose, and economic justice inside the single communities that must build it; since total harmony is the homogeneity of particular ones, and the City of Man cannot but be made of cities of men. A positive plan for world-legislation such as the sobering experiences of these decades demand cannot be assigned any longer to pure theoretical thinking, even if as masterly as Kant's, or to the magic power of dream, even if as august as Mazzini's. It must be grounded in knowledge and patience, with a comprehensive estimate of the time required by gradual adjustments and of the difficulties and resistances that must be overcome on the road to unity. Students of in-

[94]

ternational law approaching the ancient problem from contemporary angles will keep immune both to the quibbling legalistic spirit of the defunct League of Nations and to the rash, however generous, zeal of many a precursor who envisioned immediate democratic federations with the inclusion of self-styled democracies so fragile as not to withstand the first shock of war or the first impact of propaganda.

Wilson said, in the preamble to the Fourteen Points: "For our own part we see very clearly that unless justice be done to others it will not be done to us." But we for our part see very clearly that justice to others and to ourselves cannot be done through bargains and balances; that Wilson's "program of the world's peace" cannot be enforced by Leagues and courts with judges but no sheriffs. Therefore, "that program, the only possible program as we see it," even if its enactment should require the efforts of generations, is a universal law first promulgated to all humanity, entrusted to the good will of those groups and communities that are progressively disposed to adopt it, then enforced on the rebels, finally to become the common peace and freedom of all the peoples of the earth.

* * *

The four groups which we propose, while equipped with what is necessary for their purpose, should remain unhampered by the crowded staffs and the ponderous, however trivial, documentations which have "sicklied o'er" so many a reformatory intention with the pale cast of academic irrelevance.

The time accorded to their inquiry should be within the predictable limits of this decisive phase in the world-struggle—so as to make for prompt effect on action rather than for bequests to the stacks and files of a studious posterity.

One concise volume, impersonally endorsed by a company of friends, should encompass the fourfold results of this study, outlining the historic antecedents, the present terms, and the probable outlook for each of the fundamental issues, together with their convergences toward a united aim.

Such results should be meant to help pave the way toward the restoration and establishment of a systematic and integral democracy without which the challenge of Fascism and Nazism must remain unanswered except by appeasement and defeat.

Note

The foregoing DECLARATION AND PROPOSAL are the preliminary result of two years' preparation. Exchange of ideas by a small group of friends began in October 1938, soon after the surrender in Munich and the dismemberment of Czechoslovakia. It was continued through the winter and the early spring of 1939.

In May 1939—about three months before the outbreak of the second World War—the motives and intentions of this first group were summarized as follows in a

First Memorandum

May 1939

Whether it is to be war or nominal peace, the outlook in Europe, and more generally in the Old World, is anything but encouraging. If the Western powers, perhaps fortified by a more or less ambiguous alliance with Russia, will resist the forthcoming challenges of Nazism and Fascism, a conflagration may ensue with consequences as huge in immediate loss of wealth and human lives as in the probable aftermath of chaotic revolutions. If, on the other hand, a new compromise or surrender of the kind of the Munich agreement should prevent actual war, a new and more comprehensive "appeasement" might weaken to the breaking-point the lifeline of both the French and the British Empires, and certainly would magnify the influence and prestige of the totalitarian Central Powers to such a degree as to make highly questionable the preservation of what remains of independence and democracy in what is left of Europe. Less frightening, to be sure, from the immediately humanitarian point of view than the outbreak of war, this solution by appeasement would, however, be tantamount to a slow or quick death by asphyxia of practically all that we used to call civilization in the Old World. Other solutions or compromises may be kept in store by the process of history in the making; they are beyond the range of rational contemplation and the all but hopeless dilemma as formulated above seems inescapable on the basis of the predictable elements that are so far at our disposal.

The gratifying delusion that America's destiny can keep aloof from what is happening or what is going to happen in the rest of the world is vanishing at growing speed from many American minds. Whichever of the hypotheses may materialize or whichever other hypothesis may come true as the effect of new events, the shape and direction that will be assumed by Europe and the Far East together with the Empires and dependencies of European powers in Asia and Africa will affect immediately and profoundly the process of civilization and of government on this hemisphere. The problem of intervention or half-intervention or full neutrality in case of war does not concern the writers of this paper. Even if neutrality were possible during all the course of a European war, the effects of probable social upheavals following a disastrous peace would certainly react on the social organism of America so as to make defenses and counteractions of some sort inevitable. A military victory of Nazism or Fascism probably allied with Japan would certainly include a challenge of some sort, within a relatively short span of time, to the security and independence of the U. S. A. It is common knowledge at last that we live on the same planet under the same constellation of destiny and that no ocean is now broad and silent enough to keep us away from unwanted entanglements and undesirable contagions.

Therefore, whatever concerns the European nations concerns ourselves. The instruments of our attention must be sharpened, intellectual contributions to the problem of the impending future must become more operative and conscious. This duty, which is at the same time a collaboration in the service of others and a service to our own safety, becomes the more commanding the less we are entitled to expect enlightenment of a constructive kind from Europe itself. By far the largest part of the European Continent is under strict governmental control and nobody can breathe a word announcing even vaguely some hope for a future change in leadership, for a transformation of ideas, for a reformation of institutions and laws. Even on the western fringe of the Continent, where the tenets of democracy and freedom still are considered conventionally valid, freedom and democracy are modified by a growing amount of unavowed censorship and obvious fear; and all security gone from an atmosphere laden with the double threat of war and subversion, not even the finest spirits dispose of the reliance and optimism that are necessary for a collective work of restoration and progress.

In this as in many other fields the opportunity of America is unique today. We have here the necessary elements of confidence and surviving optimism, we have here, with the large number of American scholars and students of history and of political science, as of all the sciences and techniques related to politics, an exceptional selection of prominent European personalities who have left their native countries and have carried across the ocean their knowledge and their ardor, to which the adoptive country has added the invaluable gift of expression and action. The collaboration of what is best in American culture with what is best in European intellectual immigration might be the source of incalculable benefits for the active intelligence of tomorrow. There is "a time to break down and a time to build up." And even if the outlook on the events of the old Continent is gloomy, a time for reconstruction will dawn; a preparation for that time which may be remote or comparatively close must be considered as one of the main assets that the present generation can offer to itself in the next few years if destiny is lenient, or, in the worst of cases, to the coming generations. The experience of the past and especially of the recent past during and after the World War should teach us at last that there is no use in trusting the blind forces of nature and history, that a planless groping can carry mankind from the horror of war to the stupidity of improvised treaties of peace and from these to the obscurity of a wholesale disintegration. It is not Utopian to suppose that a deep, systematic, and unbiased study of the problems harassing the Europe of today, problems of political and national as well as of social, economic, and even biological nature, would mean a substantial help to the statesmen who will be called sooner or later to build a new world from these or perhaps from even more lamentable ruins.

Much of what has happened in the past twenty years is due to the action of a misled intelligentsia. It is the intellectual more than any other class that has done and undone things in Russia as in Italy and Germany. The assumption does not seem unwarranted that a well-directed intelligentsia could make up in the future for the misdeeds of the past. It becomes, at any rate, imperative to offer to the intellectual élite an opportunity to give evidence of its ability to mix in the affairs of the world, to be considered as one among the elements of leadership. Socrates in the words of Plato said that a perfect state will have the possibility of life and behold the light of day, that cities will finally have rest from their evils, "when philosophers are kings or the kings and princes of this world have the spirit and truth of philosophers and political greatness and wisdom meet in one." We do not think that the philosophers and scientists of our age will be kings and princes and we do think that their help to the building of a new society will be valuable only if they renounce all ambition of power. But it is good and necessary that they should be systematically asked about the problems that are torturing our age. It is good and necessary that at last they be offered a possibility of answering, in technical and precise terms, the questions to which no European statesmanship has been able to give answers during recent generations. At last the intelligentsia should be taken down to the earth from the midair between clouds and earth where it has hovered for centuries, content with the worship of undefined or approximately defined deities such as Justice, Freedom, Democracy, and be put to a real, steady, and substantial work through which those venerable and significant abstractions may become the pulp and nerve of practical statesmanship in a day to come. Much of the future for Europe and for all the world depends on the feeling of responsibility that will reside in human intelligence and on the authority which mankind will recognize in intelligence.

We propose the institution of a "Committee on Europe" in America. It should consist of a small number of the most prominent intellectual and political exiles from Europe and of a majority of American thinkers and scientists. The men composing the leading committee should not exceed the number of fifteen. They should be free of any allegiance except to truth and of any obedience except to the laws of this country; they should also be as free as possible of any dependence on private or corporate interests and stand as far as possible above and beyond the crystallized or crystallizing interests of classes or groups engaged in mutual strife. Their leadership should be provided with a staff of scholars and students of American and European and, possibly also, of Asiatic origin engaged in the study of particular problems. A certain number of learned refugees could find a better employment in such an organization than in the crowded competition for college and university teaching. The results of particular and general inquiries should be published in reports not signed by any single member of the board or of the staff but approved under the collective responsibility of the committee.

We trust that the work of this institution in a comparatively short time would supply the statesmen of an era of reconstruction with decisive material in all fields of national and international affairs, from the riddle of World-Government or League of Nations to the deadlock of economic class warfare, from the antithesis of authority and freedom to the relations between churches and states, to the place of family and city, to the significance and possibilities of eugenics, to the interrelation of tradition and initiative in education, and to any other larger or smaller, permanent or transitory issue, all of them needful of free and thoughtful inspection in an epoch of confusion and aimless speed.

* * *

This Memorandum was circulated among the sponsors of the "Committee on Europe" and some of their friends. New circumstances due to the imminence and the outbreak of war slowed down the progress of the project in the subsequent months.

Initiatives of a parallel kind developed meanwhile—from the end of the summer of 1939 to the end of the winter of 1940—in the interval between the Polish campaign and the subjugation of Norway. Groups of American scholars and political scientists and groups of European exiles united in divers efforts to outline plans of peace and reconstruction for the day of Franco-British victory. This day was, in the hope of many, not remote.

Even before the capture of Oslo and the battle of Trondheim, however, the small group of friends who had planned a "Committee on Europe" did not feel that the prediction of a joint Franco-British victory and of a speedy collapse of Nazism was necessarily bound to come true. They felt, besides, that these parallel initiatives did not as a rule take into sufficient consideration several of the criteria which they deemed essential.

Some of these criteria may be enumerated as follows:

1. War and its vicissitudes—which are the convulsive

expression rather than the cause of the present world chaos—should not be treated as the foundation and perspective for a plan of reconstruction. A plan of reconstruction should be such as to be held valid and adequate even if this war had been averted.

2. A redefinition of democracy and a plan for world-order should not be subordinated to the immediate issues of American neutrality or non-belligerency or intervention, but only to the basic acknowledgment that America cannot stand alone and that disaster or progress affects the world as a whole.

3. No one basic issue can be confronted in detail, apart from the other basic issues. Thus, for example, there is small hope in any plan for world-order and justice among nations which is not founded on social order and justice within the nations. Likewise, no definition or redefinition of democracy is practically or logically tenable without its premise in a statement of fundamental religious beliefs. All the converses are true.

4. There is no reason for assuming that an effort toward a redefinition of democracy and a plan for a new order will prove more successful if such an effort is confined to scholars and scientists holding academic or political

positions, to the exclusion of other categories of professions and minds.

5. It would hardly be profitable to listen to European immigrants alone, outside the frame of American thought and life.

6. Nor would it be expedient to confer a monopoly in inquiry and planning on American intellectual leadership alone, isolated and deprived of the support and aid that should accrue to it from some at least of those who have lived through the European experiences of this age.

On these grounds, the promoters of the "Committee on Europe" did not think it advisable to abandon their design. It was more definitely explained in the following

Letter of Invitation

March 28, 1940

Dear Sir:

At the beginning of the spring of 1940, after the annihilation of Poland and the surrender of Finland, onlookers see the odds divided between a devastating conflagration bursting out of the slow fire in the West and a persistent military deadlock, with plans for vaster Munichs emerging recurrently from the confusion. A third possibility—of a peace provisionally equitable, of a *modus vivendi* giving Europe opportunity for gradual adjustment and evolutionary change—may be envisioned by more confident souls. But even the best hypothesis sounds only moderately optimistic in a time of passions so strained, of interests so dramatically polarized; and such a period of transition, if it were to come to any good end, would need the assistance of all those—men of action and men of thought—concerned with the preservation and progress of our common heritage.

The first idea of an American "Committee on Europe" arose as early as October 1938, immediately after Munich, when it became clear that almost irresistible forces of disintegration were at work in Europe, with far-reaching implications for this country and the rest of the world. While this project was under consideration, initiatives of a cognate kind took shape elsewhere, especially under the pressure of the war and under the stimulus of a desire to provide governments in Europe and America with technical material for negotiations of peace. The studies and proposals of such committees and groups will doubtless be of great value; they must be taken into serious and coordinating consideration. From another point of view,

however, there might be an advantage in a different plan
—an attempt to formulate some basic principles for a
future society from which practical applications might be
deduced, leaving active statesmen and diplomats to deal
with decisions which cannot be postponed and compromises which cannot be avoided.

The forecast that our civilization is bound for a crisis
even more severe than was the downfall of ancient civilization may well sound like the overemphasis of fright-
ened imaginations. There hardly seems to be, however,
any substantial exaggeration in the statement that all the
systematic structures that have been proposed to modern
society either have collapsed or show ominous cracks. No
one worthy of being called a humanist and partaking in
the community of intelligence can feel anything but loath-
ing for the spirit of Nazism and Fascism. On the other
hand, long before the conversion of Bolshevism to a connivance with Nazism and to aggressive expansion, most
leaders in the field of intelligence wanted to keep clear
of allegiance to dogmatic Socialism as it had crystallized
in Marx's and Lenin's Communism, while the same leaders more or less passionately denounced the injustices and
inadequacies of the capitalistic order. But consensus on the
necessity of social and economic reform does not imply a
clear vision of a third road which should not take society
either to the jungle of ruthless competition or to the

prison of crushing regimentation. Likewise, the general enthusiasm for a federation to weld together all nations of Europe or perhaps of the world tends to cool as soon as the frontiers of a federal Europe are discussed, or predictions advanced on the relations, not necessarily peaceable, between a superstate, European or larger, and the states left outside, or the question raised whether it would be wise to try to build at once a house for all Europeans, or all men, on foundations still threatened by the explosives of racial rancor and class-hatred. Unanimity in the feeling that the roots of Western civilization and education are classical, Jewish, and Christian splits most sectionally when appropriate definitions are requested—especially of the third and most decisive component—or when a working outline is demanded to regulate relations between states and churches. Democracy and freedom are paramount to all thinking minds. Yet few, if any, dare confront otherwise than with noncommittal generalities the problem of a new structure strong enough to enable freedom to repulse the murderous assaults of totalitarian propaganda and conspiracy without sacrificing freedom itself in the suicidal contradiction of a fully "authoritarian democracy."

This is far from an exhaustive roll-call of the numberless issues which haunt intelligence today. None of them, obviously, is susceptible of solutions unchangeably valid in the change of places and ages, and only Utopias are perfect. Nevertheless, an approach to the possibility of a new synthesis is highly timely, even imperative. This approach should be as deliberate and courageous in intention as considerate in method. An opportunity should be offered to intelligence by which it might begin to make up for the misdeeds and mistakes of decades. Such misdeeds, in spite of all glory in the conquest of nature and of all glamour in artistic performance, were the disruptive philosophies, the indifferent sciences, the decadent aesthetics which helped to undermine the order of culture and civilization. Such mistakes were the aloofness in ivory towers or the sharpness of destructive criticism dissociated from constructive effort: an attitude of proud desertion which must be superseded by one of plain devotion neither thirsting for power nor shrinking from responsibility. Even failure in an attempt of this sort would convey to the intellectual élite a suggestion for stricter discipline in thought, while success would illumine many doubting minds and point to a better future.

We propose a first meeting of a first group interested in the building of a "Committee on Europe," such meeting to be held on three consecutive days some time in May, without any publicity before or during the meeting, and with the purpose of drafting a preliminary statement and a plan of work. Place and date will be set as soon as an-

swers to this invitation have been received. The list of the
invited is appended hereto.

*　*　*

This letter of invitation bore the signatures of G. A.
Borgese, Robert M. Hutchins, Thomas Mann, Lewis
Mumford, William A. Neilson, Reinhold Niebuhr. It was
addressed to a limited number of prospective collaborators.

Thirteen attended the first Conference. It took place
in Atlantic City from May 24 through May 26, 1940.
The first of six successive meetings was introductory, the
second dealt with war and peace and the principles under-
lying the possibility of a future world-order, the third
with definitions and redefinitions of democracy and with
the problem of the limits of freedom in discipline, the
fourth with education and religion, and the fifth with
economic reform.

It seemed to be too late, during the battle of Flanders,
for a "Committee on Europe" and on Europe alone. It
became as a temporary nucleus, without any further speci-
fication, a "Committee," tentatively, "of Fifteen."

The sixth and final meeting in Atlantic City discussed
a plan of work. A subcommittee was appointed to draft a

statement embodying the ideas and purposes that had prevailed during the Conference.

The draft was submitted three months later to a second Conference which gathered on August 24 and 25, 1940, at Sharon, Connecticut. Nine of the thirteen were present. Those who were prevented from joining the Conference, and some new friends, contributed remarks and suggestions in writing.

New members were nominated, to be invited before the publication of the statement. William Allan Neilson was elected chairman. He is assisted by an Executive Board consisting of Herbert Agar, W. Y. Elliott, Lewis Mumford, and G. A. Borgese, secretary.

The statement—or Declaration followed by a Proposal —approved as a whole by the Conference, was revised according to the suggestions expressed in Sharon, and to others made by members and friends.

The Declaration is signed and endorsed by the committee whose names appear on page 73. It is open to further endorsements.

Date Due